IMAGES
of America

NEWTOWN
1900–1960

For many years I've served ye [well?]
For many things I love it.
And though just now I feel cast dow[n]
I hope to rise above it.
1755 — 191[5]

THE CHANTICLEER, 1915. This rooster weathervane has stood on the steeple of the Congregational church since the mid-18th century except for moments such as the one captured in this photograph, when it was brought to the ground for regilding. Bullet holes, which do not show clearly in this photograph, were reputedly placed there by the French soldiers under Comte de Rochambeau when they marched through Newtown in 1781. Since they were highly disciplined troops, it was much more likely done for sport by young Newtown residents. The chanticleer has become the symbol of the town and is prominently featured on the town seal.

IMAGES
of America

NEWTOWN
1900–1960

Daniel Cruson

ARCADIA
PUBLISHING

Published by Arcadia Publishing
Charleston, South Carolina

Library of Congress Catalog Card Number: 2002111897

For all general information contact Arcadia Publishing at:
Telephone 843-853-2070
Fax 843-853-0044
E-mail sales@arcadiapublishing.com
For customer service and orders:
Toll-Free 1-888-313-2665

Visit us on the Internet at www.arcadiapublishing.com

TOWN OF NEWTOWN

THE TOWN SEAL. This rendering of the chanticleer has now been accepted as the official town seal and appears on all official stationery, documents, and business cards. The year 1705 was when the first purchase of town land was made from the local Pootatuck Indians.

CONTENTS

ACKNOWLEDGMENTS

The bulk of the photographs in this volume comes from my own collection, supplemented by those from the collections of the Newtown Historical Society. Two other collections of vintage photographs, however, were pivotal in putting this book together. Jose Rodriguez of Cartiphilian Collectibles allowed me to be the first to see a large collection of Newtown postcards of which he had just taken possession. I want to thank him profoundly for that opportunity since many of the photographs on those cards appear here. I also thank John Letson for giving me access to his Riverside photograph album and for allowing me to make copies of the many unique photographs that appear there.

Several other individuals deserve special thanks for helping secure photographs of specific locations or landmarks. Chief among these is Curtiss Clark of the Newtown Bee for photographs from the newspaper and for his general encouragement. Thanks are also due to Lilly and Tom Goosman for photographs of the Huntingtown area and for helping me identify some of the southern Newtown buildings that are now gone. I wish to thank Jodi Raymond, the postmaster of the Stevenson Post Office, and her staff for being so helpful in procuring several vintage images of Stevenson. I owe a great debt of gratitude to Joanne Brooks, who allowed me to study her photograph album of Poverty Hollow photographs taken at the turn of the century. This was the source for the photographs of the troops in Redding during the 1912 maneuvers.

As always, I wish to thank my wife, Carolyn, and sons, Daniel, Thomas, and Benjamin, who once again endured being displaced from the family room while Dad indulged his manic passion for old photographs and became grumpy over trying to find just the right words.

INTRODUCTION

In 2005, Newtown will celebrate its tercentenary. In all of its 300 years, no period has seen such dramatic change as the years between 1960 and the present. The extraordinary changes of this period, however, were conditioned by the rapid changes that occurred in the 60 years preceding 1960. Until *c.* 1900, Newtown had maintained an agricultural subsistence base with some small-scale industry. Beginning with the introduction of the automobile, the town evolved into an integrated suburban town with a highly mobile population. Using vintage photographs, this volume tells the story of that transformation.

The story begins where the town itself began, in the village, with the laying out of Newtown Street (the historical and proper name of Main Street). In 1709, the heart of Newtown was created. No matter how far into the outlying areas of town one settled, the basic amenities, such as groceries, financial services, government services, and religious worship, drew him back to the village. This continued to be true until the last three decades of the century, when commercial development in the extremities of the town (such as Sand Hill Plaza) made it easier to shop elsewhere and the creation of branch banks allowed easier financing away from Main Street. Yet, Main Street is still a main street. Newtown's citizens are still drawn to it for government services and for religious observances. The placement of its library on Main Street just south of the flagpole also draws citizens to the center of town for their education, social, and recreational needs, and the Edmond Town Hall theater still serves as an inexpensive entertainment center. The village is still the town's heart.

The story of Mary Hawley and her benefactions to the town are an important part of the changes that conditioned the present period of most rapid change. Clustered in the 12 years between 1920 and 1932, her gifts to the town transformed the landscape of the village and the immediate surrounding areas on Elm Street and Church Hill Road. From Hawley School to the Liberty and Peace Monument at the head of Main Street, Mary Hawley created the look that has greeted virtually all visitors and prospective residents. She also created institutions that continue to serve the town.

The edges of the village have served to supplement the functions of Main Street. Here developed tearooms and, with an increase in the number of automobiles, service stations. It is here, too, that the railroad was built to connect the town to the rest of the world, the first step in becoming a suburban town. Newtown's periphery was also the area selected by the state in the 1930s as the site of a premier mental health facility, which served the citizens of Connecticut for 60 years. It also served the citizens of Newtown by supplying jobs and crucial mental health services.

The second community that developed in Newtown was Sandy Hook. Here, the first mills were erected. This presaged the coming of the Industrial Revolution, which later supplied a livelihood for a great many of the town's residents. Sandy Hook also absorbed the Irish immigrants who swarmed to the United States in the wake of the Great Famine. One of the major institutions spawned by the Irish immigration was St. Rose of Lima, Newtown's Catholic church. In 1883, St. Rose settled into its permanent home on Church Hill Road, halfway between the Newtown Street vicinity and Sandy Hook, and thereby united the Catholics of both communities. The Irish of Sandy Hook gave that community a different atmosphere from that of Newtown Street and vicinity, and the social life of Sandy Hook evolved along somewhat different lines. Chapter 4 has been put together to show some of these distinctions.

Newtown developed as a town of many parts. Chapters 5 and 6 are dedicated to showing how that changed in the early years of the 20th century. As the town evolved in the early 18th century, Newtown's farmers moved into the outlying areas of the town to take advantage of the land that had been distributed to them as the town common land was being divided up among the town's first resident families. These settlers tended to build their houses close together to enjoy the companionship that comes from neighbors. In a very short time, they had created a community that centered around a one-room schoolhouse and often had its own store and small shops. The names of these communities survive today in names such as Hattertown, Huntingtown, Botsford, and Taunton even though they have ceased to function as communities. The transformation, in which the communities melded together into an integrated town, was due to two main factors. The first was the mobility that came from the growing availability of the automobile. The second was the centralization of the school system, which led to the closing of the one-room schoolhouses that had distinguished and individualized these communities. The photographs from the early years of the 20th century clearly show this transformation.

Special attention is given here to the two border communities: Stevenson, which spreads into Monroe, and Hawleyville–Land's End, which does the same into Brookfield. They share their lifestyle and topography with these neighboring towns and are therefore somewhat distinct from Newtown's other communities in that they maintain their identity in the face of the homogenization of the town's other communities.

The last three chapters continue the theme of transformation, and they were made possible by several recent discoveries. Since the first book on Newtown in the *Images of America* series in 1997, several new collections of photographs have come to light. One of these albums documents the evolution of Riverside as it changed from a summer to a year-round community. These photographs show the changes that happened from 1920 until the early 1960s and thus serve as a supplement to those Riverside photographs that appeared in the first book.

Another album was kept by a member of the New York National Guard who was involved in the 1912 war maneuvers that culminated in the center of Newtown. They supply a rare personal look at those maneuvers and give a close-up view of the U.S Army in the pre–World War I period. These have been combined with some other recently discovered photographs that show the movement of troops in Redding and some other surrounding towns to create a chapter that considerably clarifies the story of those maneuvers.

Finally, images from a recently discovered cache of postcards have allowed a chapter that has been called simply "More Special Events." Although this chapter stands on its own to give the reader a feel for the special nature of Newtown, when viewed with the photographs of the previous book, it allows a deeper understanding of what makes Newtown a true community in itself. Newtown may have grown into a suburban town, but the special events of first half of the 20th century have created a small-town atmosphere that still lingers and attracts many new residents.

One

THE VILLAGE I: MAIN STREET, THE HEART OF THE TOWN

NEWTOWN FROM THE AIR, 1935. This view of Main Street was taken as part of an aerial survey of Connecticut. In the center, the Congregational Meeting House can be seen in the middle of West Street. The large oval at the bottom is the remnant of the old Newtown Fair racetrack (1896–1906). The northern portion of this track can still be seen today north of Taylor Field.

A QUIET RURAL VILLAGE, C. 1905. Here is the western side of the village as it would have been seen almost 100 years ago from Castle Hill Road, just before it begins its climb up the steepest part of the hill. Castle Hill Road joins West Street where the road disappears from view in the distance. The large structure above that intersection is the Newtown Inn, which was replaced by the Cyrenius H. Booth Library in 1931.

THE CENTER OF TOWN, C. 1970. This familiar panorama of the town's center was taken from the top of Castle Hill and features the flagpole and the two oldest churches in town. In the early 1970s, a third steeple was added to this scene with the construction of the new Congregational church. The back of the Yankee Drover, which burned in 1981, can be seen through the trees to the right.

MAINTAINING NEWTOWN STREET, C. 1910. This road grader had to be used frequently to refinish the dirt-and-gravel surface of Main Street. This was one of the best roads in town, but the *Newtown Bee* is filled with complaints about its condition, especially in the spring, when heavy rains eroded its surface and turned the shoulders into a quagmire.

A PERMANENT SOLUTION, 1928. Finally, in 1928, a permanent solution was found to Newtown Street's continuously poor condition. Here, concrete is being poured onto a base of gravel. This concrete still exists beneath the bituminous macadam that the state now uses to finish the road surface.

NEWTOWN STREET BEFORE AUTOMOBILES, C. 1905. The street just north of the flagpole is shown here in the days of the horse and buggy. When the new Edmond Town Hall was built in 1930, the house to the extreme right was taken down. Also taken down was the building to the left of the house that had served as the Newtown Academy, a Catholic church, and the Newtown Town Hall.

HONAN'S FUNERAL HOME, C. 1910. These two houses stand on the west side of Newtown Street slightly north of where the last photograph was taken. To the left is William Honan's residence, and to the right is the house that was turned into a funeral home by Honan's father in 1912. The senior Honan was one of the first undertakers to embalm the deceased in this area.

THE GLOVER HOUSE, 1905. Recently placed on the National Register of Historical Places, this house is a superb example of the Second Empire style of architecture. It was built in 1869 by Henry Beers Glover, one of the founders of the Newtown Savings Bank, which has served the financial needs of Newtown since 1855. Glover's descendants continued to live in this house until 1977.

Newtown, Ct.
9-23-06

Success to you, Harris
Send along a card as often as you can find time.
Jewell

"JIMMIE."

THE GLOVER THIRD GENERATION, 1905. Florence and Marguerite Beecher, the granddaughters of Henry Beers Glover, are seen here in a pony cart hitched to their horse Jimmie in front of the Glover house. Florence lived in this house from 1918 until her death in 1977. Because she married Steven Budd, the house has been known to the present generation of Newtown residents as the Budd house.

Residence of F. J. Naramore, Newtown, Conn.

A FEDERALIST MASTERPIECE, 1914. Built by David Curtis in 1791 on the corner of Main Street and Church Hill Road, this house is one of the best examples of the High Federalist style of architecture in town. Curtis ran the first general store in Newtown directly across the street, where Flag Pole Realty is today. That first store still survives as the little florist shop in the rear parking lot.

THE FIRST TOWN HALL, 1910. The second building from the right has been known recently as the Scudder Building or simply as the Brick Building. It was constructed in 1845 to house the town clerk and probate offices. Town meetings were held upstairs. The staircase on the building's right was the only access to the second story, since the building did not have an internal staircase until recently.

Congregational Church, Newtown, Conn.

Pub. by Danziger & Berman, New Haven, Conn.

THE CONGREGATIONAL CHURCH, C. 1920. The first church stood in the middle of the intersection, where the flagpole is now. In 1792, it was moved to its present location, in the middle of West Street, to make room for the new Episcopal church across the street. This building, now called the Congregational Meeting House, was built in 1808 and was extensively rebuilt between 1845 and 1852.

GILDING THE TOWN'S ICON, 1939. This snapshot shows two men on the Congregational church steeple. The one on top is Burt Nichols, who has just regilded the chanticleer (rooster) and is replacing it. The man at mid-steeple is his son and assistant Al Nichols, who was Newtown's postmaster from 1941 until he retired in 1979.

15

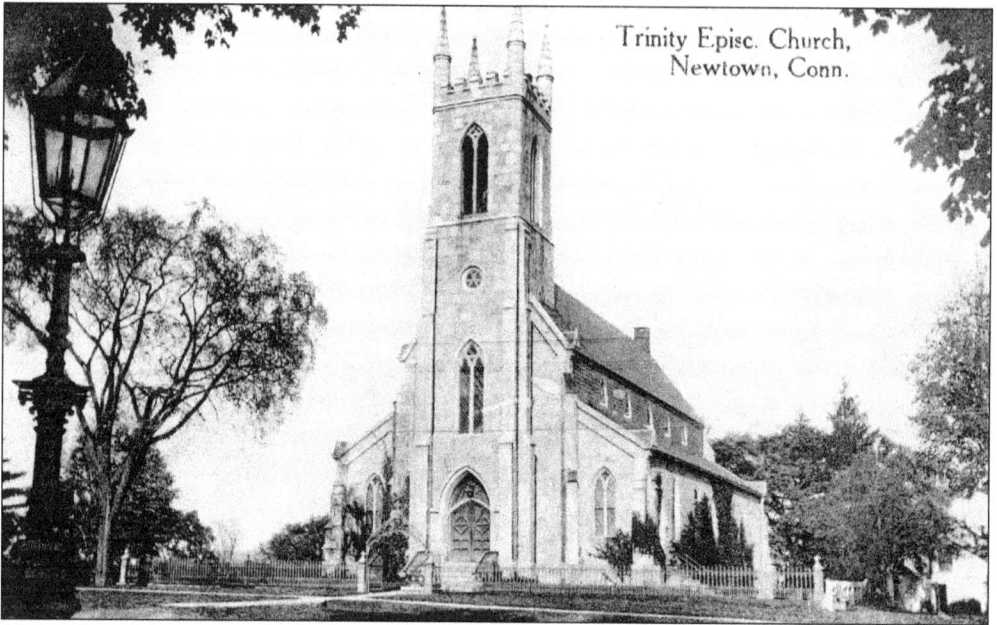

TRINITY EPISCOPAL CHURCH, 1915. The second Trinity Episcopal Church was built in 1792 and stood in the middle of Church Hill Road. (The Congregational church across the street is one of the only churches still standing in its original position in the middle of a street.) In 1870, this stone building was constructed just south of the old wooden structure, and the old church was demolished.

TRINITY EPISCOPAL CHURCH, 1950. This view of the north side of the building clearly shows the Gothic windows and raised clerestory with the smaller arched windows. When this building was constructed in 1870, the Gothic revival was in its last stages, but the Gothic style had a firm hold on the imaginations of the church's building committee.

TRINITY EPISCOPAL CHURCH, c. 1915. The Gothic style is carried into the church's interior, as can be seen in this rare early photograph of the church. The high pointed arches that separate the wide central aisle from the two side aisles is in direct imitation of the large stone cathedrals of 12th-century Europe.

TRINITY EPISCOPAL CHURCH, C. 1920. This closeup of the altar area was taken just before an Easter service in the early 1920s. The photograph shows this area before the pulpit was built in the left altar rail.

THE FIRST BANK, C. 1915. The Newtown Savings Bank opened for business on September 15, 1855, in the front room of Henry Beers Glover's house. It continued operating out of private homes until this building was reconstructed in 1871. It then moved into the rooms on the right side of the building, on the ground floor. It remained here until the bank built its own building in 1909.

THE NEWTOWN SAVINGS BANK, C. 1920. Constructed in 1909, this was the first bank building in town. It underwent major renovations in 1954 and again in 1964, but the stone building pictured here still survives. It is hidden by the walls of the later additions.

18

THE NEWTOWN SAVINGS BANK, 1909. Construction of the Newtown Savings Bank building began as all commercial ventures, with a portrait of the bank officers ready to break ground. The men seen here are probably the bank's president, David C. Peck, and one of its vice presidents, either Daniel Beers or Philo Nichols. The man to the right appears to be the treasurer, Arthur T. Nettleton.

THE NEWTOWN SAVINGS BANK UNDER CONSTRUCTION, 1909. Before the days of bulldozers, this is the way a foundation was dug. The house just behind the horse team is the old Congregational church parsonage, which is today part of the bank building.

THE NEWTOWN SAVINGS BANK UNDER CONSTRUCTION, 1909. In this view, the foundation has just been laid and the basement windows set in. Recently, while undergoing the latest renovation, these foundation stones were uncovered in the basement of the present bank building.

THE NEWTOWN SAVINGS BANK UNDER CONSTRUCTION, 1909. By August 1909, the building was beginning to take a familiar shape. The facade seen here was a familiar sight on Main Street until the renovation of 1964.

THE NEWTOWN SAVINGS BANK INTERIOR, 1909. This is the view that greeted all visitors to the newly constructed bank in 1909. The man behind the teller's cage is Arthur Treat Nettleton, who guided the bank's affairs as treasurer from 1898 until 1938. He served as a combined treasurer and president from 1938 until shortly before his death in 1951.

THE NEWTOWN SAVINGS BANK, 1955. The first major renovation of the bank occurred in 1955, the centennial of the bank's formation. At that time, a large addition was extended out to the rear of the old building, almost doubling the building's square footage. The interior was also completely redone, as can be seen in this view facing the main entrance.

THE NEWTOWN SAVINGS BANK INTERIOR, 1964. The second major renovation was completed in 1964. The house to the south of the bank had been purchased and demolished. The building was then pushed out to the south, and again the interior was modernized. (Compare this photograph to the previous one, which was taken in the same position.) The tellers' cages were moved to the other side of this main room. (See the next photograph.)

THE NEWTOWN SAVINGS BANK, 1964. This image was taken by turning 180 degrees from the last one. It shows the tellers' cages and the mural that was commissioned for this renovation. The mural still graces the main room after the most recent renovation (2001). Note that the entrance to the vault is in the center of this photograph, in the same position as it was in 1909.

THE BEERS-TITCOMB HOUSE, C. 1900. This stately Colonial house was built in the last decade of the 18th century and stood just to the south of the bank building. The building to the right is the old Newtown Academy, which was moved before 1909. This is now the location of the bank parking lot. The demolition of this house created a controversy that resulted in the creation of the Newtown Historical Society.

THE CONGREGATIONAL CHURCH PARSONAGE, 1929. Built in the early years of the 19th century, this building housed the church's ministers until the 1970s. It was recently purchased by the bank to make room for its latest renovation. The building was demolished, and constructed in its place was a replica, which now houses bank offices.

THE NEW HOME OF THE NEWTOWN BEE , 1905. The *Newtown Bee* was founded in 1877 and was printed for 26 years in the upper story of the Chase Block (see the upper photograph on page 18). The newspaper moved here to its new home in 1903. This view shows the newly constructed building decked out in bunting for the 1905 town bicentennial parade.

THE RENOVATED NEWTOWN BEE BUILDING, 1950. This photograph shows the Newton Bee building after two major renovations. The second one pushed the building out to the east and more than doubled its square footage. Whereas Main Street is the heart of Newtown, the *Newtown Bee* is its brain. It still remains a vital source of information on the town.

THE BEACH MEMORIAL LIBRARY, C. 1925. This was the first permanent library building. It was built in 1900 with money donated by a descendant of Rev. John Beach, the first minister of Trinity Episcopal Church. It was converted into a house in 1932 after its function as a library was superseded by the Cyrenius H. Booth Library. The building still stands just opposite the entrance to Hanover Road.

THE MARYLAND TEAROOM, 1930. The Maryland was a short-lived tearoom that stood on the southeast corner of Main Street and Glover Avenue. It was best known for its chicken dinners. By 1932, it had been converted into a house, which still stands diagonally across from the Pleasance (a private park).

THE SHEPARD RESIDENCE, C. 1915. A good example of the Italianate architectural style, this house has occupied the northeast corner of Main Street and Glover Avenue since just before the Civil War. It housed five generations of the Shepard family including, presumably, the one pictured with the boulder, which marks the spot where the first Episcopal church service was conducted in 1732.

THE CENTER OF TOWN, C. 1920. The flagpole marks the geographical and emotional center of Newtown. This is the town's third flagpole, erected in 1914 and replaced by the present steel pole in 1950. This landmark has resisted numerous attempts by the state's department of transportation to have it moved, and most directions to anywhere in the northern county begin with "Start at the flagpole."

26

Two

THE VILLAGE II:
THE HAWLEY FACTOR

THE VILLAGE CEMETERY, 1924. Mary Hawley was the town's benefactor. Among her benefactions was the beautification of the old village cemetery. In addition to landscaping, she rebuilt Hawley Lane, with its picturesque bridge, had the gates and fence installed, and had the holding vault built that can be seen in the center of this photograph. This view is unchanged today except that the vegetation is overgrown and the graves are more numerous.

MARY HAWLEY, C. 1925. This formal portrait is one of only five known photographs of Mary Hawley. She was born in 1857 in Bridgeport and moved to Newtown with her parents in 1872. After a short disastrous marriage, she led a reclusive life with her mother. In the decade between her mother's death in 1920 and her own death in 1930, she made three major gifts to the town, including Hawley School, the entrance to the village cemetery, and Edmond Town Hall. When her will was read, it was found that she had posthumously bestowed two more gifts on the town: the Cyrenius H. Booth Library and the Liberty and Peace Monument. Her house became the Hawley Manor restaurant and inn and most recently the Inn at Newtown.

MARCUS HAWLEY (1834–1899). Marcus Hawley was the father of Mary Hawley. He had followed his father in the hardware business and made his fortune supplying hardware to miners during California's gold rush. Seeing the potential of the country's fledgling railroads, he invested heavily in them, increasing his fortune until he became one of the wealthiest men in Fairfield County.

SARAH HAWLEY (1830–1920). Sarah Booth Hawley was the daughter of Cyrenius H. Booth, a noted physician in mid-19th-century Newtown. She married Marcus Hawley in 1856. When her father died in 1871, she convinced her husband to move to Newtown after extensively renovating the doctor's old house, more than doubling it in size. Marcus Hawley then commuted daily to his offices in Bridgeport and New York on the railroad.

THE HAWLEY SCHOOL, C. 1925. After Newtown High School burned in 1920, Mary Hawley was convinced by her financial adviser, Arthur T. Nettleton, to donate the money to build a replacement. The building was completed in 1921 and, for many years, was considered one of the most advanced school buildings in the state. Contrary to modern mistaken opinion, the school was named after her parents. It was not named after her.

THE HAWLEY SCHOOL ADDITION, C. 1950. The original building accommodated almost all of Newtown's schoolchildren from first grade to twelfth grade. By the end of World War II, however, as Newtown's population began its precipitous rise, the building became crowded. This addition was added to the rear of the building, but not before the crowding became so bad that some of the old one-room schoolhouses had to be reopened.

THE EDMOND TOWN HALL GROUNDBREAKING, 1928. Even before ground could be broken, the old firehouse had to be moved. This old building had served as a town garage and jail before being pressed into service for Newtown Hook and Ladder. In 1933, this building was replaced by the present structure in the rear parking lot of the town hall.

THE EDMOND TOWN HALL FOUNDATION, 1928. A substantial building needs a substantial foundation. Shortly before this photograph was taken, the old town hall, which stood just in front of this foundation, was taken down. Once that was done, these excavations began. The modern steam shovel to the left is a definite improvement over the horse team used when the Newtown Savings Bank was built (see page 19).

THE EDMOND TOWN HALL BASEMENT, 1929. Once the reinforced-concrete foundation was poured, the brickwork could begin. The brick wall seen here is the back wall of the basement gymnasium. The building also had a bowling alley, courtroom, offices for the town clerk and probate court, a movie theater with the capability of showing sound films, and quarters for the post office. (The post office is now the first selectman's suite.)

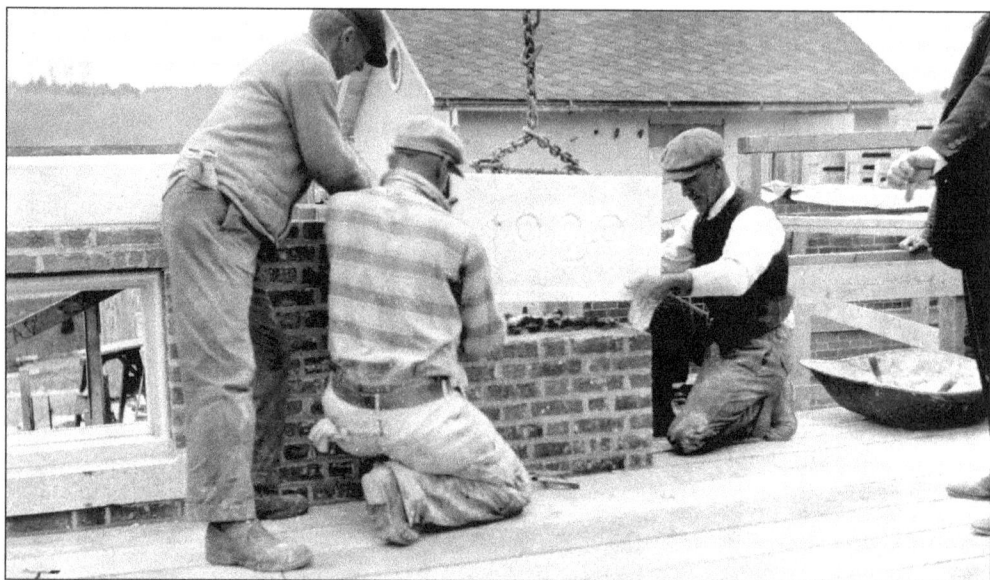

THE EDMOND TOWN HALL CORNERSTONE, 1929. On May 1, 1929, the cornerstone was ready to be set in place. This became an occasion for celebration. Everyone who was important in town gathered on that chilly, rainy day to watch Mary Hawley place a trowel full of cement on the bricks that would receive the stone. In this photograph, Hawley has just stepped out of camera range to the right.

32

THE EDMOND TOWN HALL ARISES, 1929. By late 1929, the building was beginning to take on its recognizable shape. At this point, Mary Hawley had become ill. Everyone offered prayers that she would live to see the building completed. This was not to be. As her funeral cortege slowly made its way to the village cemetery, the bell in the town hall steeple tolled for the first time.

THE EDMOND TOWN HALL COMPLETED, 1930. The completed town hall is seen here with its windows open to allow the fresh paint in the interior to dry. The building in the foreground is the old meat market and post office. Shortly after this photograph was taken, the building was taken down to make room for the exit driveway of the town hall parking lot.

THE CYRENIUS H. BOOTH LIBRARY, C. 1932. It was not until Mary Hawley's will was read that Newtown residents knew she had provided them with money and land for a new library. This was originally the site of Dick's Hotel and, later, the Newtown Inn. The old inn was cut into pieces and moved to various locations on Main Street to be used as outbuildings.

CYRENIUS H. BOOTH (1797–1871). The only known photograph of the library's namesake was used to make this 1929 engraving. Booth came to Newtown in 1820 and practiced medicine until his death. Once it was renovated, his house and office (where the Inn at Newtown is today) became the house in which Mary Hawley spent most of her life. (Booth's house still survives in the walls of the inn.)

THE LIBRARY CIRCULATION DESK, C. 1932. The new library, like Hawley School, was a state-of-the-art facility that contained cork floors and acoustic ceiling tiles to deaden sound. It even had a centralized vacuuming system so that a custodian only had to carry around a short length of hose and plug it into a baseboard connection to clean the rooms. All of the light fixtures were also custom made.

THE LIBRARY READING ROOM, C. 1932. Most of the furniture was custom made for the library, including the extraordinarily comfortable leather couch seen here. In addition to serving as a library, the building was also used to display Mary Hawley's dining room and bedroom furniture. A room on the second floor and another in the attic are still maintained as her dining room and bedroom, respectively.

THE LIBERTY AND PEACE MONUMENT, 1931. Also discovered in Mary Hawley's will was money for a monument to honor the town's war dead. Franklin L. Naylor was contracted to design the monument, and his design was executed by the McGovern Granite Company of Hartford. This photograph shows the new monument at its dedication in 1931.

THE LIBERTY AND PEACE MONUMENT, 1940. This striking Baisley postcard shows the monument under simulated night conditions. Because the lists of Newtown's soldiers and sailors are inscribed on bronze plaques placed around the base of the monument, it has become popularly known as the Soldiers and Sailors Monument.

36

Three

THE EDGES OF THE VILLAGE: THE HEART'S PERIPHERY

JEANVILLE, C. 1915. In the late 19th century, some of the town's wealthier residents began to settle away from Main Street, on its periphery. An outstanding example is the classic Queen Anne–style house constructed by I.B. Harris in 1889. This house stands on Route 302 just west of its intersection with Main Street. The reason he called his estate Jeanville is unknown.

THE JOHNSON HOMESTEAD, C. 1900. This substantial farmhouse once stood on South Main Street across from Ricky's Shopping Center. It was built in 1830 by Charles Johnson. His son Ezra was born and brought up in this house and continued to here until his death in 1914. Ezra Johnson is honored today as Newtown's first historian.

EZRA L. JOHNSON (1832–1914), 1900. This is obviously not Newtown. Ezra Johnson was a well-traveled man. This photograph was taken at Balancing Rock in Colorado on one of his many trips to the West. In addition to being Newtown's historian, he also taught school in Newtown's district schools and served on the board of school visitors (a forerunner of the board of education) for an unprecedented 58 years.

THE JOHNSON MILL, C. 1900. This mill served to grind grain and press cider for the Johnson family throughout the 19th century and into the early 20th century. It was located in the southern end of Queen Street at the Mile Hill Road intersection. The overgrown foundation can still be seen just off Queen Street. The mill was taken down in 1979.

THE MILLPOND, 1910. The pond for the Johnson mill was created by a dam on Deep Brook at the Queen Street and Mile Hill Road intersection. The pond extended to the south and west almost to Ricky's Shopping Center. The road shown here is an abandoned portion of South Main Street, which led to the mill from what is today Route 25.

THE SOUTH CENTER SCHOOLHOUSE, C. 1920. Photographs of the South Center School are rare. This one shows its placement at the intersection of Elm Drive (left) and South Main Street (right). Classes ceased here in 1922, and the building was sold in 1927. It was eventually moved by Wilton Lakeye and placed behind his Sandy Hook house just south of St. John's Church on Washington Avenue, where it still stands.

AMARAL'S SERVICE STATION, 1937. Serving the automotive needs of Newtown since 1933, this service station was opened by Tony Amaral (left) on the corner of South Main Street and Borough Lane. Amaral became a dealer for Chrysler automobiles and is shown with three of the latest models. He continued to sell Chryslers until his death. Today, the business continues under the guidance of his sons Dan and Marcus Amaral.

EXPANSION ALONG CHURCH HILL ROAD, C. 1920. In the early 20th century, in addition to mansions and business the periphery of the village began to fill with upper-middle-class residences such as these along Church Hill Road west of the intersection with Queen Street. Most of these houses have now been converted into business offices or have been torn down to make way for commercial buildings.

NEWTOWN'S FIRST MOVIE THEATER, C. 1920. Movies had been shown in the old town hall since 1896, but the first theater dedicated to movies was this building, situated across from St. Rose. The photograph was taken just before the building was converted to a theater. The theater showed silent films with piano accompaniment. In 1931, however, it reverted to a service station because the theater could not compete with Edmond Town Hall, which was equipped for talkies.

41

THE NEWTOWN DEPOT, 1880. This is the earliest known photograph of Newtown's second depot, shown just after it was built in 1880. It burned 10 years after this photograph was taken and was rebuilt exactly as it is shown here. The railroad made Bridgeport accessible for shopping trips and even commuting for people like Marcus Hawley. This was Newtown's first step toward becoming a suburb.

THE NEWTOWN DEPOT, C. 1930. Shortly before the beginning of the 20th century, the long platform canopy was added to the depot. An occasional freight train still passes this station, but it does not stop. Passenger service ceased over half a century ago. The building now houses a comic book shop and small restaurant.

THE BORDEN CREAMERY, 1936. Owned by the New York, New Haven, and Hartford Railroad, this building was leased by the Borden Milk Company and served as a point to which farmers could daily bring their milk for transshipment to Borden's processing plants. The creamery opened in 1902 but, by 1914, shrinking usage forced Borden to shut it down. At the height of its business, the creamery served more than 80 farmers.

NEWTOWN Conn. R.R. Station

A DISASTER AT THE DEPOT, 1959. For unknown reasons, a southbound freight jumped the track as it passed by the station and proceeded over the trestle. Although boxcars hung over the road at the trestle, none fell onto oncoming cars and no one was hurt. Traffic on the line was held up for over two days.

FAIRFIELD HILLS, 1934. In the early 1930s, the state picked five farms along Mile Hill Road to become the site of its new mental health facility. The first building phase included the construction of the three buildings around the entrance to the complex—Newtown, Woodbury, and Shelton Halls. Pictured here is Shelton Hall before the two large Y-shaped wings were added to each end of the building.

FAIRFIELD HILLS, C. 1940. In the center of the hospital complex is Bridgeport Hall. This immense H-shaped structure served as the kitchen and dining facilities for almost all hospital personnel and patients. Once the hospital closed in the early 1990s, the town arranged to purchase the complex. The fate of Bridgeport Hall is uncertain, but it will probably continue to serve as the venue of the library's gigantic Labor Day book sale.

THE LITTLE BROWN HOUSE, 1925. The Little Brown House billed itself as a motor inn and tearoom. It was one of several such establishments that developed in rural Newtown to serve the growing popularity of automobile day trips into the country. It opened in 1924 and was very popular, serving more than 275 dinners in July and August. It is uncertain when it closed, but it survived at least three seasons.

THE TEAROOM INTERIOR, 1925. Photographs of tearoom interiors are extraordinarily rare. This view of the Little Brown House interior shows the establishment's Spartan but homey atmosphere. The tearoom was located on the boulevard about halfway between Church Hill and School House Hill Roads. Now a private home, it is still brown.

MOUNT PLEASANT, 1910. The tearoom craze developed as automobiles became affordable and common in the 1920s. Vistas such as this one attracted automobile drivers to venture on day trips into the country. Once in the area, the visitors would break for lunch at a local tearoom. This view is at the top of Mount Pleasant, looking back toward the hill that drops down into Newtown Street and vicinity.

ANOTHER MOUNT PLEASANT VIEW, 1910. This view shows another rural vista from the top of Mount Pleasant, with Route 25 running off toward the horizon. With the farmhouse, fields, stone walls, and almost unimpeded views in all direction, the area was quintessentially bucolic.

MOUNT PLEASANT, THE WINTER OF 1920. In contrast to Mount Pleasant in the summer is the mountain in the winter, when the road had to be kept clear to allow the passage of essential traffic. Before snowplows, shoveling was a common method of keeping the main roads clear. The photograph was taken by William Johnson, who was the highway supervisor in Newtown and was responsible for hiring this crew.

A COFFEE BREAK ON MOUNT PLEASANT. Another Johnson photograph shows part of the crew stopping for warm coffee and a bite to eat. These men were clearing snow after the heavy blizzard of February 20, 1920. When this photograph was taken, they were working at the top of Mount Pleasant about a mile from the northern end of Main Street.

AN ANTIQUE CONVEYANCE ON MOUNT PLEASANT. This is why the shovel crews were working to clear the road. By 1920, sleighs such as this were rapidly dying out in favor of automobiles with chains. During blizzards, however, the sleigh was often returned to the road, if its owner still had a horse. Note that the shovel crews did not clear snow all the way to the gravel road surface. (Hard paving did not occur here until the early 1930s.)

Four

SANDY HOOK: BUSINESS AND SOCIAL LIFE

St. Rose's Rectory, Newtown, Conn.

THE ST. ROSE RECTORY, C. 1930. With the rapid influx of Irish immigrants in the 1850s, the need for Catholic services became increasingly acute. St. Rose was organized in 1859, and masses were conducted in the old town hall on Main Street. The church was finally moved into its present home on Church Hill Road in 1883, and this rectory was constructed for Fr. Patrick Fox in 1895.

THE ST. ROSE RECTORY AND CHURCH, C. 1920. This photograph, taken in the early 1920s for the purpose of making postcards, shows the proximity of the rectory and the old church. The rectory still looks the same as it does here. It is one of the few buildings in the St. Rose complex that has not changed dramatically.

ST. ROSE CHURCH, C. 1920. The 1883 church was built halfway between Sandy Hook, where the predominant population of Irish had settled, and Newtown Street and vicinity, where a smaller number of them had established themselves. Therefore, the church's location served to tie together the two populations. This building was done in the neo-Gothic style, which was in waning popularity at the time it was built.

ST. ROSE CHURCH, 1911. The Gothic style of the exterior matched that of the interior in the same way it did in Trinity Episcopal Church (see page 17). The pointed arches and groin-vaulted ceiling are even more Gothic here than in Trinity. This church was torn down in 1954 to make way for the larger present structure.

THE ST. ROSE COMMUNITY HALL, C. 1930. St. Patrick's Hall, St. Rose's first parish hall, was built on this site to the rear of the church in 1879. It was enlarged and modernized in 1928, at which time it was renamed St. Rose Community Hall.

SANDY HOOK CENTER, 1929. The business center of Sandy Hook begins at the base of Churchill Road. The most prominent buildings here are some of the few that have escaped the frequent fires that plagued Sandy Hook at the start of the 20th century. In the foreground is the Sandy Hook Hotel (Troy Hotel), built in 1832. Just behind it is the Sandy Hook Drug Store, built in 1878.

Main Street, Sandy Hook, Conn.

SANDY HOOK CENTER, C. 1955. Sandy Hook has not changed much since this photograph was taken half a century ago. The drugstore in the foreground was built by Dr. William C. Wyle to supply his patients. Wyle later became internationally famous for his medical journal. In 1909, the drugstore became Corbett and Crowe, which remained in operation until the retirement of Arthur "Doc" Crowe in 1953.

52

SANDY HOOK CENTER, C. 1910. This view, looking back up Church Hill Road, illustrates a more dramatic change in the Sandy Hook business district than does the previous view. The mill to the left was built in 1842 as a satinet factory. (Satinet was a fabric made from a mixture of wool and cotton.) It was rebuilt in 1881 as the Niantic Mill, which manufactured woolen garments. It later recycled old wool called shoddy—hence, the origin of the word for something of poor quality.

SANDY HOOK CENTER, C. 1935. The Niantic Mill was torn down in 1926 by Austin Hurd and was replaced by a service station (blocked from view by the post office). The post office was constructed in 1905 after the previous building was destroyed by fire. In 1970, the post office moved into the building next door and this building remained vacant until it was torn down as an eyesore in 1982.

THE GOLDEN PEACH, C. 1920. In 1916, Jack O'Neil came to Sandy Hook from New York. Leasing this building from Edward Troy, who ran the hotel two doors west of here, he fitted it out as an ice-cream parlor that almost immediately became very popular part of Sandy Hook's social scene. When O'Neil died in 1923, the business was taken over by Steve Wargo.

THE GOLDEN PEACH, 1928. Under Steve Wargo, the Golden Peach moved across the street to the building shown here. It is uncertain exactly when the business ceased, but it was still in operation in 1930. After it finally closed, the job of supplying ice cream fell to Arthur "Doc" Crowe, who built a soda fountain in his drugstore across the street. The building seen here is now a restaurant called 100 Church Hill Road.

THE RED BRICK STORE, C. 1950. A general store has operated on this site since William B. Glover opened a business here in 1833. In 1857, the original building was moved across Church Hill Road, and this brick store was constructed. This business continued under a number of different partnerships to serve the mercantile needs of Sandy Hook until 1978, when Hawley Warner, its last proprietor, retired.

THE WILLIAM B. GLOVER RESIDENCE, C. 1950. This beautiful Italianate house was constructed for William B. Glover in 1861. Glover had amassed a great deal of wealth as the proprietor of the red brick store on the other side of Glen Road. In the 1950s, the building was adapted as a tourist home, as seen here. Most recently, it has been converted into offices.

Dayton Street Bridge,
Sandy Hook, Conn.

THE DAYTON STREET BRIDGE, 1915. This highly controversial bridge was built in 1890 to connect the north end of Dayton Road with Glen Road. It was constructed to make the route shorter for the residents at the end of Dayton Road who worked in the rubber factories. This bridge has been restored as an unusually good example of a late-19th-century through truss bridge.

A VIEW FROM THE DAYTON STREET BRIDGE, 1909. Standing on the Dayton Street bridge and turning 90 degrees south, one gets this view of Sandy Hook and the Pootatuck River. The prominent building to the left is the rear of the red brick store. The dam across the river diverted water to run the gristmill on Glen Road, about 500 feet north of the store.

THE METHODIST CHURCH, 1917. The first Methodist service was held in a private home in 1800. By 1831, the Methodist congregation was prosperous enough to buy a building that stood just north of Marcus Hawley's residence (the old Hawley Manor). The building seen here was constructed in 1850 on the corner of Dayton Street and Church Hill Road to accommodate its ever growing congregation.

THE METHODIST CHURCH, 1972. A large crowd turned out to watch the old Methodist church being moved across the street to its present location. The move was made in order to give the church room to expand and add a parish hall. In 1967, to accommodate the move, Fredricka House, a Sandy Hook landmark and former summer residence of stockbroker Edmund Gibson, was torn down.

ST. JOHN'S CHURCH, 1914. Although St. John's did not become an independent parish until 1880, this church building was constructed in 1869 and functioned as a chapel of Trinity Episcopal Church until parish status was obtained. The new parish was formed to give better local service than could be obtained by a church in the village. The building to the left is the Masonic hall, built in 1905.

ST. JOHN'S CHURCH, C. 1930. On the night of December 27, 1929, a fire destroyed the old wooden building. Almost immediately, funds were raised to replace the old structure with this one, built predominantly in stone.

ST. JOHN'S RECTORY, 1909. This house, located on the lower part of Church Hill Road and now gone, served as the residence of St. John's rectors from the time of the formation of the parish. When this photograph was taken, it housed Rev. Otis O. Wright (1891–1912), who became one of the most popular of Newtown's clergy. He established the Sandy Hook library and was deeply involved in the town's public schools.

ARTHUR "DOC" CROWE, 1944. Arthur Crowe (right) first came to work in the Sandy Hook Drug Store in 1904, when it was run by Betts and Betts. He went into partnership with Martin Corbett in 1909 to become Corbett and Crowe. During the war, he collected photographs of Newtown's servicemen and displayed them in back of the soda fountain. The man with him is soda jerk Charles Lockwood.

THE SANDY HOOK GIANTS, C. 1930. The Sandy Hook Giants played teams from all of the surrounding towns in the Western Connecticut League. They played at Pine Grove Park in Sandy Hook (now under Route 84), a farm field that they converted into a baseball diamond. The team was managed by George Clark Sr. Clark's son George Jr. (kneeling in front) served as water boy and bat boy, and supplied this photograph.

THE LILLIS AND HURD SERVICE STATION, C. 1925. Lillis and Hurd ran one of the first permanent service stations in Sandy Hook. In 1922, after having worked at another unknown location, they opened in this building. Four years later, Auston Hurd went on to tear down the Niantic Mill and constructed his own service station on the site. The business pictured here continued under several owners and is now run by Adolph "Junior" Dreher.

THE UPPER RUBBER FACTORY, C. 1870. Hard-rubber goods were first made in this converted cotton-spinning mill in 1855, after it was taken over by Conrad Poppenhusen. Poppenhusen ran this factory until 1863, but it was forever after known as the Dutch Rubber. The New York Belting and Packing Company acquired the plant in 1863, and it was converted to recycle rubber. The building seen here burned in 1887 and was replaced with the present brick building.

THE LOWER RUBBER FACTORY, C. 1870. Rubber products were first produced on this site as early as 1844. When the New York Belting and Packing Company acquired the company in 1856, it turn to making rubber cloth and industrial belts. The year the company purchased the plant, it burned and was replaced by this larger brick structure. This industry gave employment to many Sandy Hook men until it closed in 1977 and Fabric Firehose, the last tenant, moved to North Carolina.

GALLAGHER'S STORE, 1925. Located on the eastern end of Glen Road, this establishment supplied food and supplies to many of the summer residents who lived along the upper end of Lake Zoar. After World War II, building became a drinking establishment, and its reputation deteriorated. On February 18, 1973, Tuttle's Glen Lodge, as it was then known, was destroyed after eight intensive hours of firefighting. Arson was suspected.

THE SANDY HOOK RAILROAD STATION, C. 1920. This station was located on Glen Road just a few hundred feet from the bridge across Lake Zoar. It was built by the New York and New England Railroad to connect the rail hub at Hawleyville to Waterbury. The existence of this line ensured the success of the rubber factories, since it supplied an inexpensive means to ship goods and raw material.

THE SANDY HOOK RAILROAD STATION, 1927. Another view of the Sandy Hook station shows its relationship with Gallagher's Store. This station was taken over by the New York, New Haven, and Hartford Railroad in 1900. After World War II, the line was discontinued and, in 1949, the tracks were torn up.

THE GLEN ROAD BRIDGE, C. 1920. This bridge was built at the end of the 19th century to replace the wooden bridges that were yearly damaged by spring ice floes. This photograph shows a frozen Lake Zoar and the bridge-damaging ice. In 1933, this bridge was replaced by the current one.

THE SANDY HOOK RAILROAD BRIDGE, C. 1915. The bridge seen here replaced an earlier wooden one when that bridge caught fire and was destroyed in 1905. This fireproof steel bridge continued to facilitate the movement of goods back and forth to Waterbury until just after World War II. It was dismantled in 1949, the same year that the tracks were taken up and the Sandy Hook station was abandoned.

BENNETT'S BRIDGE, 1918. Bennett's Bridge was so named because the Bennett brothers built and maintained a bridge here in the late 18th and early 19th centuries. This is one of the last photographs of the bridge before it was submerged under Lake Zoar in 1919. The Man wistfully contemplating the doomed bridge is Frank Johnson, a brother of William Johnson, who took this photograph.

Five

THE OUTLYING COMMUNITIES: MANUFACTURING AND FARMING

THE PALESTINE DISTRICT SCHOOL, C. 1930. The outlying communities centered around their one-room schoolhouses. The Palestine District was created as early as 1748. However, this one (the second school) was built in 1883 and was one of the last to close, in 1936. Until that closing, the area around it found its identity in the school, and even the news of this area was listed under the heading "Palestine" in the *Newtown Bee*.

TAUNTON LAKE, 1910. One of the first communities to develop away from the village was Taunton, which centered around the northern end of Taunton Lake. The Taunton school district was created in 1738 and lasted until 1934, at which time school-age children walked or rode the bus to Hawley School in the village. The closing of the district school marked the end of Taunton as a distinct community.

TAUNTON LAKE, 1909. The lake made Taunton a popular place to spend a summer vacation. In the 19th century, small houses along the northern and western shore of the lake were rented out, creating a minor resort area. During the off-season, however, these houses were often rented to individuals who had a different sense of recreation, and the northern end of the lake developed a reputation for extreme moral laxity.

BOTSFORD HILL, 1911. In the early 1950s, a controversy raged over the name of this road. One faction claimed it as part of Botsford; another wanted it to be called Toddy Hill. Today, this house is at 115 Toddy Hill Road. A short distance down the road, by the entrance to Button Shop Road, the addresses are Botsford Hill Road.

BOTSFORD HILL, 1911. This is a rare photograph of the Sunrise Hotel, which stood on Toddy Hill Road at the entrance to Ashlar. Previously known as the Broadview Hotel, it reopened as the Sunrise Hotel in 1919 and was closely tied to the Jewish community in Huntingtown. It often held fund-raisers for the synagogue on Huntingtown Road and frequently housed vacationing New York City Jews who were looking for a week or two in the country.

BOTSFORD HILL, 1949. Even before World War II, the Sunrise Hotel's business declined. In 1937, the hotel was sold to the East Side House. Under the new ownership, it became known as Camp Stepney and supplied an opportunity for inner-city children to experience the country. This barn, which housed the game room and craft workshop, still stands on the corner of Toddy Hill Road and Settler's Lane.

BOTSFORD HILL, 1949. The dining hall for Camp Stepney was the restaurant section of the old Sunrise Hotel, shown here ready to serve a camper's lunch. This image and the previous one came from postcards that were sent by Patsey Ward to his city-bound mother.

THE SKIFF SUMMER SCHOOL OF MUSIC, 1914. This postcard and one other are the only evidence that this school ever existed. Even the ubiquitous *Newtown Bee* does not contain any reference to it. The building shown here is no longer in existence, and the only mention of a Professor Skiff is to a concert he conducted in the old town hall in 1914.

THE BOTSFORD STATION, 1924. The real center of Botsford was the railroad depot that once stood on the bend of Botsford Hill Road. This area was originally call Cold Spring, but after the Civil War, it was renamed Botsford for Oliver Botsford, who served as postmaster here from 1849 until 1883. This view shows the east side of the depot. The tracks run on the other side.

THE BOTSFORD STATION, C. 1910. Another view of the depot shows the small freight office in the foreground. This station was abandoned after World War II, but the abandoned building stood here until it was destroyed by arson in the early 1990s. Then, all that remained of the railroad's presence here was the old water tower. That was dismantled and moved to the railroad museum in Danbury in the late 1990s.

A SCENE FROM THE BOTSFORD POST OFFICE, C. 1925. Several times a day, someone sitting on the front steps of the post office, which was in Albert Rasmussen's store, would be treated to a scene like this. The scene became increasingly rare over the years. Today, only four freight trains a day pass here, usually at night.

70

FROM THE BOTSFORD STATION, C. 1905. This photograph was taken from the platform of the freight building, looking north. The post office and store can be seen in the distance, and the 90-degree bend in Botsford Hill Road is to the left. The shot was taken before the underpass was dug out to eliminate the dangerous grade crossing seen to the left.

THE BOTSFORD POST OFFICE, 1905. Albert Blakeman built this store, post office, and residence in 1893. His brother Austin Blakeman served as postmaster until 1910, when the store and post office was turned over to Lawrence Taylor. The longest term as postmaster here can be claimed by Albert Rasmussen, who held the position after Taylor from 1919 until 1961, when the post office moved to Route 25.

THE HUNTINGTOWN STORE, C. 1910. Just as Botsford's economy centered around its store, so did Huntingtown's. This store served the community on lower Huntingtown Road at the end of the 19th century. In 1909, the store and neighboring house were purchased by Jacob Goosman, at which point the store was used for storage and occasionally rented out to summer vacationers.

THE HUNTINGTOWN STORE, C. 1915. This building, at 99 Huntingtown Road, sits diagonally across the road from the site shown in the last photograph. It was opened as a store by Samuel Nalvens in September 1910. By 1928, it had been acquired by Morris Levenson, who continued to do business here until his death in 1962, after which it became a private residence.

THE HUNTINGTOWN DISTRICT SCHOOL, C. 1925. The students seen here are mostly children of the Jewish immigrants who came to the lower Huntingtown valley in the early years of the 20th century. The teacher to the left is Ruth Roberts, who taught here from 1921 until the school closed in 1941. The school was reopened between 1944 and 1949 to accommodate the sixth grade until the Hawley School addition could be built.

THE GROUNDBREAKING FOR THE SYNAGOGUE, 1914. The spiritual center of Huntingtown is its synagogue. It was built in stages on land donated by Israel Nezvesky, beginning with the groundbreaking in 1914. The cornerstone was laid in 1919, and the building was dedicated in 1920. The rabbi house is across the street and was the old schoolhouse (see above), which was converted into a dwelling in 1950.

73

SOPHIE'S TEA HOUSE, C. 1925. Just as in the village, teahouses began to appear all over town in the 1920s to cater to day-tripping motorists. This little teahouse was located on Route 25, just south of the junction with Washbrook Road and was operated by Sophie Kraepelin between 1923 and 1929. It was then sold to James Solen, who converted it to a full restaurant, renaming it the Pines.

THE PINES RESTAURANT, C. 1940. In 1935, John Hansen bought the Pines and completely renovated it. The restaurant's specialty became the copyrighted "Picknichicken." The restaurant became a popular meeting place for Botsford residents, and local institutions, such as the Botsford Fire Department, had their origin here. The Hansens sold the establishment in 1950, and it rapidly deteriorated. It was destroyed by fire in 1963.

74

THE CROWE-KEANE BUTTON FACTORY, C. 1910. Just a short distance north of the Pines on Route 25 was this button factory. Established in 1844, it was one of the earliest of Newtown's button shops. In 1870, it was taken over by Patrick Keane, who ran it until his untimely death in 1896, after which the business was taken over by Keane's nephew Patrick Crowe.

THE CROWE-KEANE BUTTON FACTORY, C. 1905. By the time of the 1893 depression, virtually all of Newtown's button manufacturers either had gone out of business or had turned to making other products. Crowe-Keane weathered the storm and continued to produce buttons until a fire destroyed the plant in 1926. The remains of the sluiceway that led water to the plant's waterwheels can still be seen on Route 25 across from Sand Hill Plaza.

HATTERTOWN GREEN, C. 1920. Another Newtown community that grew up around manufacturing was Hattertown which, as the name implies, was a center of hat production. The community focus is this green, across which runs Castle Meadow Brook, seen to the lower right. The road that curves south here is Hi Barlow Road, named for Hiram Barlow, who lived at its southern terminus.

THE GREGORY'S ORCHARD SCHOOL, C. 1900. Hattertown was the popular name for the community. Its formal name was Gregory's Orchard, the name of the school district. This school was the educational and social center of the community. It once even served as an impromptu courtroom. The teacher here may be Miss Brockett of Bethel, and the young scholars come from the Mayer, Summers, Morgan, and Paprowski families.

THE HIRAM PARMELEE HOUSE, 1917. Hiram Parmelee was a well-known carpenter of the mid-19th century. He built churches in Redding, Newtown (Congregational), and Brookfield. While building the latter church, he fell and was slightly injured. He then made his living as an undertaker and maker of coffins. The house still stands at 174 Hattertown Road, and the building to the left is his carpentry shop.

HATTERTOWN GREEN, 1907. The road that passes off to the west (left) here is Hattertown Road. The house to the left still stands on the corner on Hattertown Road and Aunt Park Lane. The Gregory's Orchard School, in its original location, can be seen peeping through the trees to the left of the house. Morgan's Store, the building to the right and now gone, was the mercantile center of Hattertown.

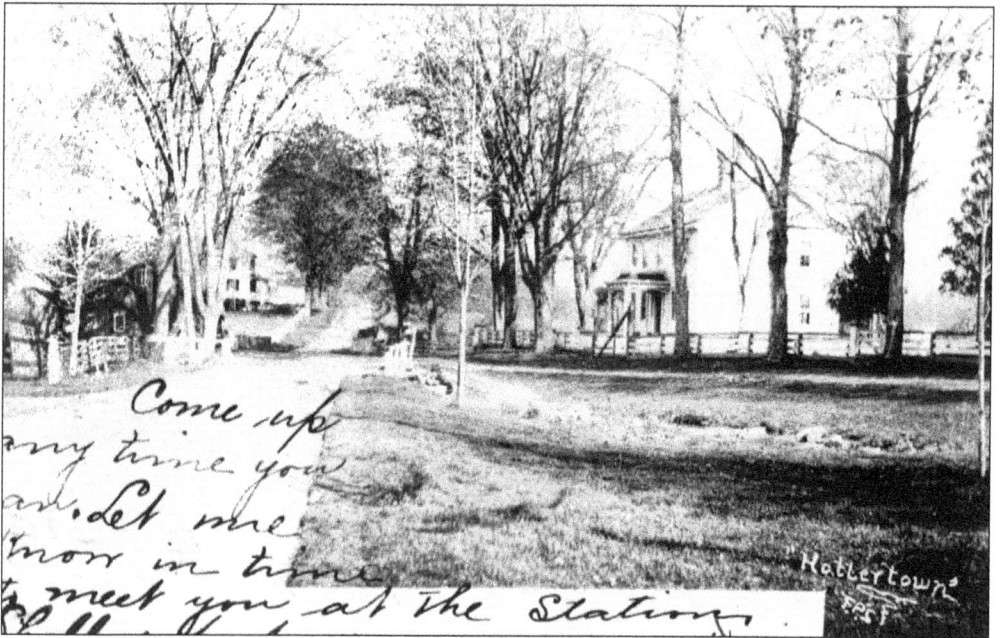

HATTERTOWN GREEN, 1907. Hattertown Road runs to the east here toward Stepney. The house in the center of this view is the Elam Benedict house, named after its most important resident. Elam Benedict came from Danbury in 1921 and introduced hatting to the community. His granddaughter Celestia Benedict received her doctor of medicine degree from the Woman's College of Pennsylvania in 1874 and became one of the first female doctors in the state.

HATTERTOWN GREEN, 1907. This view of the southeastern corner of the green has changed very little. The house to the extreme right in the Levi Taylor house, which is the oldest house in the area, dating from 1750. To the left is a small outbuilding with an advertisement on its side. Foster Kane Clothiers of Bridgeport painted its name on any standing structure that it could find in Newtown at the beginning of the 20th century.

GRAY'S PLAIN, C. 1910. This photograph was taken on Route 34, looking north toward the entrance of Zoar Road, which is just around the bend. Gray's Plain was a farming community that was much less prosperous than Hattertown. The little one-and-a-half-story house to the left is typical of the modest farmhouses that characterized these farming communities, and it is one of the few that have survived.

THE GRAY'S PLAIN SCHOOL, 1890. This is one of the few surviving vintage photographs of the Gray's Plain School. The woman to the left of the window is the teacher, Elizabeth Wheeler, who shortly after this photograph was taken, became Mrs. Homer Clark and left teaching. The girl to her left is Agnes Ryan, who became a highly controversial teacher at this school five years after this photograph was taken.

ARCADIA FARM. After her marriage, Elizabeth Clark (née Wheeler) moved down Route 34 to Arcadia Farm, shown here. The house, much altered, still stands across from the entrance to Great Ring Road. On August 12, 1912, this farm became the center of a major battle between the red and blue armies during the war maneuvers of 1912 (see chapter 9).

THE CLARK-BURR MEAT WAGON, C. 1910. Several times a week, Homer Clark would load this wagon with freshly butchered meat and carry it on a circuit around the southern Newtown. With a scale in the back, he would cut meat to order for the housewives he visited. Clark holds the reins of Spot. Dick is eclipsed by Spot. Part of Clark's circuit was Stevenson, one of Newtown's border communities.

Six

THE EDGES OF TOWN: STEVENSON AND HAWLEYVILLE

THE ZOAR SUSPENSION BRIDGE, 1919. This bridge stood just south of Newtown in Monroe, and it became a landmark for Stevenson. It was built in 1876, six years before the same technology would be employed to build the Brooklyn Bridge. This photograph was taken less than a month before the bridge was destroyed. When Lake Zoar flooded the Housatonic Valley, the towers ended up 10 feet underwater.

SMITH'S STORE, C. 1910. This store stood on the east side of Zoar Bridge in Oxford. One of the cables can be seen running into the bridge abutment in front of the building. The Zoar Bridge Post Office was also located here, but it was replaced by the Stevenson Post Office when the railroad was completed through Stevenson in 1888, making the delivery of mail faster and less expensive.

THE ZOAR SUSPENSION BRIDGE, C. 1910. The Monroe entrance to the bridge can be seen here over the horse pulling the photographer's wagon. Note the sign that prohibits trotting on the bridge, since the bridge moved as animals passed over it. The value of such a bridge was this ability to move and thus not be destroyed by ice floes, as several previous wooden bridges had, during the spring breakup.

STEVENSON DAM UNDER CONSTRUCTION, 1919. Building Stevenson Dam was a complicated process. A small semipermanent barracks was built for the workers who labored for more than two years on the project. Seen here are the small generating facility that provided electric power during construction and the plant where the immense amounts of concrete needed for the dam were mixed.

STEVENSON DAM UNDER CONSTRUCTION, 1917. An early coffer dam and bridge was constructed to allow men and machines to move easily from one side of the river to the other. More than two years were spent in construction from this point before the dam was closed on November 24, 1919, and Lake Zoar created.

STEVENSON DAM UNDER CONSTRUCTION, 1919. A small narrow-gauge railroad was built to facilitate the movement of goods and men over the entire area of construction. The small locomotive seen here was the primary means of moving the loaded cars. Rumors persist that when the project was over and the dam closed, this locomotive was left behind and that it still sits in 60 feet of water.

STEVENSON DAM, 1920. The newly completed dam can be seen here in its entirety. The loss of Zoar Bridge was compensated for by placing the road (Route 34) on top of the dam. The upper story of the Connecticut Light & Power generating plant, the reason for building the dam, can be seen to the right, as can a recently returned World War I soldier who is looking over the new landmark.

THE FIRST STEVENSON DEPOT, C. 1900. Stevenson received its name for Col. William Stevenson, who as president of the railroad was responsible for creating the extension that connected Derby to the Housatonic Railroad at Botsford. When the line reached the Monroe-Newtown line in 1888, Stevenson erected this depot and arranged to have the post office moved here from Oxford, giving identity to this border community.

THE SECOND STEVENSON DEPOT, C. 1910. When the first depot burned in 1905, this second one was quickly built. It resumed being the center of the Stevenson community, along with the Burr-Twist store, to the right. This store also contained the transplanted post office.

THE BURR-TWIST STORE, C. 1910. The store and post office's role as a social center and gathering place can be clearly seen here in what appears to be a flag raising, possibly for a Fourth of July celebration. This building is now a private home, and the post office has moved across the street.

THE HEART OF STEVENSON, C. 1910. With the depot to the left and the Burr-Twist store just visible to the right, the social and business center of Stevenson can be taken in at a glance. The building in the center of the photograph was a feed store. According to the sign on the side of the building, it was also a distributor for Adriance Buckeye mowers.

SHOWING OFF FURS, C. 1910. Trapping was an activity that was pursued by many Newtown residents who lived in the outlying areas of town. It was especially popular with the town's young people, for whom the furs supplied spending money in the days before allowances. Trapping activity remained popular here until well after World War II. The school in the background is the Half Way River School.

THE HALF WAY RIVER SCHOOL, C. 1910. The Half Way River formed the boundary between Newtown and Monroe and gave its name to this little one-room school, even though the building was entirely in Newtown. It originally stood on Route 34 (the road to the right) just south of Jordan Hill Road. This view looks south along Route 34.

THE HALF WAY RIVER SCHOOL, 1909. This typical class photograph shows how small the student populations in some of the outlying one-room schoolhouses could be. There were only 16 students registered in 1909, the year this picture was taken. The teacher was Elsie M. Gilbert, and her charges came from the Beardsley, Clark, and Eichler families who lived in Newtown and Monroe.

THE LOVELAND MILL, 1909. The business centers of the outlying communities were often their sawmills and gristmills. This was the case for Stevenson, where the brothers Giles and Grover Loveland operated this mill on the Half Way River. This river once marked the northern boundary of Stratford, and it supposedly derived its name from its position halfway between Stratford center and Woodbury, which was an outpost in interior Connecticut in the 17th century.

CAMP LIFE ALONG LAKE ZOAR, 1929. With the creation of Lake Zoar, there were suddenly abundant opportunities for recreation. Vacation and summer homes began to be built along the shore (see Riverside in the next chapter). Camps like this one were set up to allow city folk to unwind from their frenetic lives while roughing it in the country.

BUCOLIC STEVENSON, C. 1920. One of the main attractions of Stevenson were marvelous rural scenes. Two children are walking along a dirt road while several boys sport in the water of a cove, newly formed by the flooding of the Housatonic valley to create Lake Zoar. This road leads to Point Lookout, where there is a marina today.

SAMUEL B. BLACKMAN'S STORE, C. 1905. At the opposite end of town is Hawleyville, which is centered around the railroad station and this local landmark. The building was constructed in 1891 by A.G. Baker, who used it as a retail outlet for his furniture. After Baker's death in 1901, S.B. Blackman turned part of the building into a general store.

THE HAWLEYVILLE LACE FACTORY, C. 1910. Beginning in 1902, Blackman leased out the main section of the building to a lace curtain manufacturer. One of the attractions of this building for businesses was its proximity to the railroad. Five separate railroad lines, running 153 trains a day through Hawleyville, offered abundant opportunities for shipping products almost anywhere. Hawleyville was a major rail hub.

90

UPHAM FOOD PRODUCTS, C. 1920. William Upham discovered the value of Hawleyville's railroads in 1916, when he took over this building and began manufacturing peanut butter. World War I made it difficult to secure the needed peanut oils, so he turned to other foods. In 1919, just before this picture was taken, he invented the tea bag and made a substantial fortune on this novel and convenient way to package tea.

UPHAM'S JAPANESE TEA GARDEN, C. 1930. In 1928, Upham dredged a lake behind the house seen here and turned it into an oriental garden. He opened the house as a tearoom and also as a place to display his extensive collection of Chinese and Japanese furniture and antiques.

UPHAM'S JAPANESE TEA GARDEN, c. **1930.** In 1930, William Upham extended the lake and built an island that was connected to the mainland with rustic bridges. In the center of that island he put an 18-hole miniature golf course. The house and the remnants of this lake can still be seen on the west side of Route 25 just north of the railroad tracks.

THE HAWLEYVILLE CHAPEL, c. **1910.** Early in 1897, a group of neighbors decided they would built a nondenominational chapel. They agreed to locate it just north of the house that Upham eventually turned into his tearoom. They were ready to dedicate the building by December 1897. The last service held here was a funeral in 1937. After that, it was used for a number of commercial purposes over the years.

LAND'S END SCHOOL, 1905. Although the business area was referred to as Hawleyville after several prominent members of the Hawley family, the area was also known as Land's End after the school district. Land's End School was known for its large enrollments. This view shows 26 students, but enrollments as high as 45 were not uncommon. The teacher is Cornelia Morehouse, seated in the center of this student cluster.

LANDS END COUNTRY STORE

LAND'S END SCHOOL, C. 1952. Because of the large enrollments, lack of room at Hawley School, and the expense of transporting students from this extreme end of town, Land's End School was the last to close. Its students were finally sent to Hawley School after the 1948 addition was built. In 1952, the building was sold to the neighboring Clark family, who ran an antiques store there until the mid-1960s.

THE TURNER MILL, C. 1900. Gristmills and sawmills could be found on Pond Brook wherever there was a sufficient drop of water. This mill, which belonged to Joe Turner, was located at 18 Obtuse Road. It operated for a short time as a carriage factory in the 1860s, but its primary function was always a gristmill. In 1943, it was purchased by Herman DeVries and was turned into a dwelling house.

THE TURNER MILLPOND, 1909. The dam for the Turner mill was located just south of the building. Stretching to the south of that was the pond seen here, with a picturesque farmhouse and outbuilding on its banks. The dam was breached and the pond drained in 1950, but the farmhouse and barn are still there.

Seven

FROM SUMMER COMMUNITY TO YEAR-ROUND LIVING: RIVERSIDE

THE BEGINNING, C. 1925. Riverside began with the creation of Lake Zoar. By 1920, when the lake reached its full depth, new recreational opportunities were created, and Riverside was developed to take advantage of these. This view from the end of Riverside Road shows the western abutment of Bennett's Bridge (see page 64), which is all that is left of that pivotal river crossing.

MISS RIVERSIDE, C. 1930. In the early 1920s, Soule-Roberts Inc. of Bridgeport purchased a large parcel of real estate on the banks of the newly formed lake and began subdividing it into small lots on which summer cottages could be built. *Miss Riverside* was used to take prospective buyers out on the lake for a general pleasure ride and to see from the water the lots that they might want to purchase.

A RIVERSIDE OVERVIEW, C. 1930. This overview of the Riverside community was found in a recently discovered album that photographically recorded the summer community *c.* 1930. The building in the foreground is the community house and, on the distant hillside, there is a typical cluster of cottages. To the left, just to the right of the lower branch of the tree, Olmstead's Pavilion and the waterfront are barely discernible.

THE COMMUNITY HOUSE, C. 1930. This building was the heart and nerve center of the community. It was a place to meet and talk with other denizens of the summer settlement, which is what the figures sitting under the shadow of the wraparound porch are probably doing. This was also the location of a common well from which water could be pumped for use in a nearby cottage.

THE COMMUNITY HOUSE INTERIOR, C. 1930. The small community house consisted of only one principle room. The well-used fireplace and grouping of chairs speak eloquently of the social functions of the building. The flashlight on the table was a necessity after dark, since Riverside did not have electrical service in the first decade of its existence. Many individual cottages did not have power until after World War II.

RIVERSIDE UNDEVELOPED, C. 1920. This photograph, taken during the spring before the leaves were on the trees, shows Riverside as yet undeveloped. It focuses on a lone house, which was all that occupied this promontory in the year after the dam was closed and the lake created.

RIVERSIDE DEVELOPED, C. 1930. The same view taken some 10 years later shows dramatic growth. The same house is still there in the center of the image, but it is almost entirely hidden by a tree. A new road has been cut where before was only an access path. The most notable change is the grouping of cottages on what was once a bare farm field.

COTTAGE CONSTRUCTION, C. 1930. Once a lot was purchased, it was up to the owner to arrange for the construction of the cottage. Here, the lot owner and a couple of friends see to the framing of a vacation dwelling while the rest of the family camps next door. A striped canvas privy stands just behind the skeletal cottage.

CONSTRUCTION COMPLETED, C. 1925. This is a typical Riverside summer cottage, fitted out with a front porch and a cobblestone chimney, which was characteristic of 1920s construction. The fireplace that was served by this chimney was needed for cool summer nights and the occasional weekend stay in the spring or fall.

CONSTRUCTION COMPLETED, C. 1930. The most desirable cottages were those close to the edge of the lake. This lakeside summer home shows the front porch and chimney that were characteristic of most of the Riverside cottages, but it also shows some major differences in layout from the cottage in the previous photograph. There was a suggested pattern of cottages that could be built, but they all tended to be mildly idiosyncratic.

RIVERSIDE WATERFRONT, C. 1925. The waterfront was the principle attraction at Riverside. Although all cottages (even the interior ones) had access to the lake via a common beach, many of the cottages that were right on the water had their own private access, even though the climb down to the water might be a little precipitous.

LORENZO'S, C. 1928. There were three refreshment stands where some basic supplies could be obtained in addition to a hot dog and a coke. This one, built in 1928, is located at the corner of Riverside Road and Center Street and survives as Lorenzo's Restaurant. This stand is now the front section of the restaurant building, where the bar is located.

LORENZO'S, C. 1940. A large addition made to the original refreshment stand allowed for the creation of a dining room. This photograph, looking toward the front of the building, shows the main room. Lorenzo's became best known for its pizza.

PAPA LORENZO AT WORK, C. 1940. Louis Lorenzo prepares one of the night's many meals. The son of Italian immigrant Joseph Lorenzo, who moved to Bridgeport c. 1909, he was the man responsible for turning a hot dog stand into a restaurant. During the 1950s, he operated this restaurant only in the summer and spent his winters in Florida.

A TYPICAL SUMMER SCENE, C. 1925. With the awnings out and cars parked nearby, this is a scene that would have greeted any summer visitor. Most of these cottages were uninsulated and unheated except for an occasional fireplace, so they were not suitable for winter living.

RIVERSIDE IN THE WINTER, C. 1930. In startling contrast to the previous photograph, this one shows deserted cottages and snow on the ground. In the period after World War II, many of these cottages had adequate heating installed and the walls were insulated and finished with wallboard. This marked the beginning of Riverside as a year-round community.

RIVERSIDE IN THE WINTER, C. 1930. Winters were colder in the 1930s than they are now. Lake Zoar stayed frozen most of the winter, and that afforded an anonymous photographer the opportunity to walk out onto the ice to record this Riverside winter panorama.

RIVERSIDE AS WILDERNESS, C. 1930. One of the advantages that Riverside enjoyed, aside from access to the lake, was its remoteness. When you negotiated its dirt roads to get to your cottage, you were literally getting away from it all. As many of the early summer residents have recently remembered, getting into Riverside along a winding dirt road was like an excursion into the wilderness. This nameless Riverside road, wild though passable, exemplifies the image that early residents harbor in their memories of the community's remoteness.

104

Eight

MORE SPECIAL EVENTS

THE NEWTOWN BICENTENNIAL, 1905. Photographs of the 1905 bicentennial parade, marking the 200th anniversary of the purchase of Newtown from the Pootatuck Indians, are very scarce. This is one of only two known photographs of the parade's floats. It shows the Newtown Bee's entry waiting for the parade to step off at the old fairgrounds (now Taylor Field). The front page of the *Bee*, with portraits of the bicentennial's organizers, adorns the wagon's sides.

THE NEWTOWN BICENTENNIAL, 1905. All of the buildings along the parade route were decked out in patriotic bunting. Two photographs of these buildings have survived—the Newtown Bee building (see page 24) and this commercial building complex known today as the Chase Block. The left-hand portion was R.H. Beers general store. The small figure standing to the right of the store is probably R.H. Beers.

RALLY DAY, 1922. The reasons for Rally Day are not at all clear. The local papers merely stated that it was an attempt to boost membership participation at the local Congregational church, especially for the Sunday school. The event was deemed important enough, however, to pose the entire Sunday school in front of the side wall of the church and issue the image as a postcard.

THE WELCOME HOME PARADE, 1919. As troops returned from World War I, many towns had parades welcoming them home, and Newtown was no exception. Here, local nurses, some of the first women to formally serve in war, march by the flagpole on their way to the reviewing stand in front of the old town hall. They are followed by Newtown's new war veterans.

NEWTOWN'S LATEST VETERANS WELCOMED HOME, 1919. Newtown's soldiers and sailors are seen a little more clearly here as they march into position before the old town hall. After executing another right turn, they will take up their position of honor on the raised dais in front of the building.

THE WELCOMING COMMITTEE, 1919. These patriotic young girls honor the troops as a now forgotten dignitary addresses the assembled crowd. The man with the top hat and spats to the left is Patrick H. McCarthy, who taught at the North Center and Land's End Schools for more than 30 years before becoming Newtown's postmaster.

THE VETERANS ON DISPLAY, 1919. After the patriotic young girls have stepped back, Newtown's war veterans are clearly visible in their place of honor.

MEMORIAL DAY, 1930. The honors conferred in the preceding images continued every Memorial Day with a parade. The parade in 1930 is seen here as it comes through the railroad underpass in front of the depot. The Girl Scouts seen here had just been organized by Agnes Cullens at the end of 1929. They were the female counterparts of the Boy Scouts, who had been organized by her husband, Paul Cullens, in 1928.

MEMORIAL DAY, 1929. The parade of the previous year had seen Newtown's Boy Scouts march for the first time. Also in that parade was this troop of Sea Scouts from New Haven. (Newtown did not have a Sea Scout group until 1934.) The focus of the day's activities was the little triangle where the Liberty and Peace Monument was erected in 1931 (see page 36).

THE WASHINGTON BICENTENNIAL, 1932. After the celebration of the town's bicentennial in 1905, the next major celebration with matching parade was held on July 1, 1932, to honor George Washington. (This was when the first Washington quarters were issued.) Here, a float for the Quaker Farms School passes in front of the Newtown Savings Bank, followed by one of Newtown's first fire trucks.

THE WASHINGTON BICENTENNIAL, 1932. The parade continues with floats passing a bunting-covered Edmond Town Hall, which had opened the year before. The lead float (just behind the horses) carried Frederick Stoddard impersonating George Washington and William Johnson as Abraham Lincoln. This was one of the few floats that was pulled by horses (donated by the 4-H). Joe's Shop follows, representing the local farrier (horseshoeing blacksmith).

110

THE WASHINGTON BICENTENNIAL, 1932. Although a few floats were pulled by horses, ridden horses have always been part of Newtown's parades. Unfortunately, the identity of these riders has been lost, but they appear to be forerunners of today's Newtown Bridal Lands Association.

THE WASHINGTON BICENTENNIAL, 1932. The parade route went from Main Street up Mount Pleasant to the driveway of the Cole (later Gretsch) property and ended at the Castle Ronald. Here, on the front lawn, all of the town's children were assembled and given American flags. This massive flag rally was the final tribute of the day to George Washington on the bicentennial of his birth.

SILVER CITY, 1960. In the late 1950s, a local tourist attraction in the form of a Wild West town was developed on Hanover Road, just south of Silver City Road. This is the main street (and only street) of the ersatz town. Obviously not a single special event, this somewhat seedy attraction was special for many young people who visited it.

SILVER CITY, 1960. A 90-degree turn from the previous view shows the rest of Silver City's main street, including the marshal's office and jail, the stable, the blacksmith shop (with a small corral in front), and the western half of the Silver City Saloon. In front of the corral and saloon, periodic gunfights were staged for the visitors. More sedate pony rides were also available for young visitors.

SILVER CITY, 1960. No Wild West town is complete without an Indian settlement, and Silver City's consisted of a small grouping of tepees placed on the hillside above the Main Street. Periodically, over the course of a weekend, the Indians would get out of hand and attack the town. With tourists walking into their houses, it is not surprising that the Indians got a bit grumpy. The girl is identified only as Jane.

SILVER CITY, 1960. Once every Sunday, the local authorities would have trouble with the Dalton Brothers. They would always shoot at least one of the brothers, but they would be careful to capture one and put him in jail. A lynch mob would then liberate the prisoner long enough to hang him from a tree. Yes, that is a real person, and he is being saved from strangulation by a parachute harness.

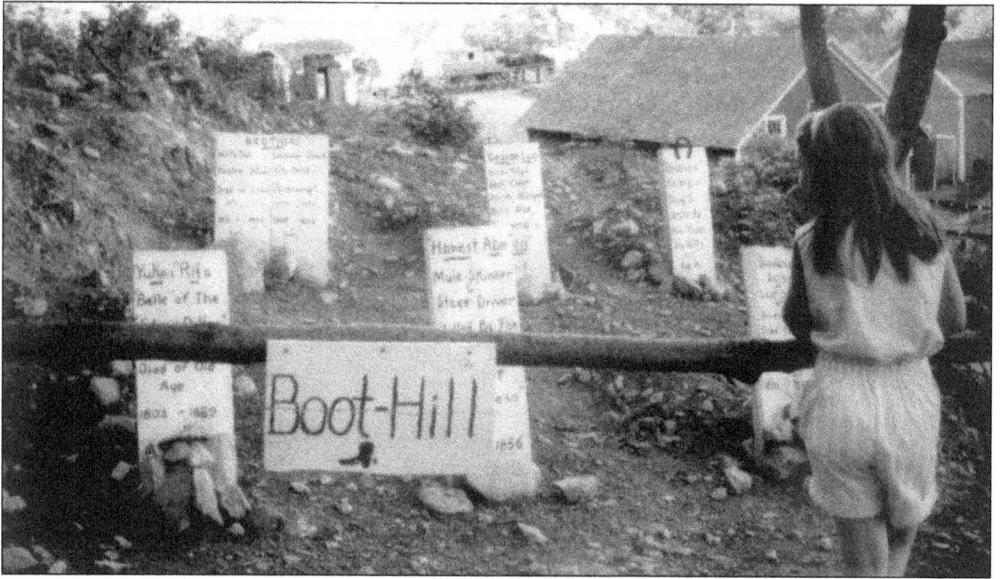

SILVER CITY, 1960. Here is Jane again, this time contemplating her mortality at Boot Hill. Silver City reached its peak of popularity in the summer of 1960, when it attracted great hoards of local tourists. By the end of that year, however, the town was abandoned, the victim of financial mismanagement. The last remnant of the town, the Silver City Inn, was destroyed by a suspicious fire in 1971.

THE CREATION OF THE NEWTOWN HISTORICAL SOCIETY, 1963. The most important special event of the period covered here is the formation of the Newtown Historical Society. The men who conceived of the society and gave it birth are, from left to right, Tom Cheney, a local attorney; Paul Smith, the editor and publisher of the *Newtown Bee*; Louis Untermeyer, poet and anthologizer; and Frank Johnson, grandson of Newf town's first historian, Ezra Johnson.

Nine

NEW LIGHT ON THE WAR MANEUVERS OF 1912

THE OPENING GAMBIT. Identified here only as musician Stanhope, this bugler is issuing a call to action. The object of these maneuvers was to have the red army, about 10,000 troops stationed in New Haven County, attack and capture New York City, defended by the blue army consisting of another 10,000 troops stationed in central and western Fairfield County. The objective of the red army was later refined to capture the Croton Reservoir and thus New York.

CAMP LIFE. This is the red army's Camp No. 3, which was located on the Half Way River in Stevenson. These photographs are part of an album put together by an anonymous member of the New York militia (later called the National Guard). He was apparently part of the red army, which had advanced from New Haven County, crossing on the old Zoar Bridge on its way north and west toward the Croton Reservoir.

THE COOK TENT GOES UP. The most essential part of any camp is the cook tent. Here, the tent is being put up. The album consisted to a great extend of photographs of camp life, which is a subject most easily photographed because of the relatively sedentary and slow nature of camp activities.

READY FOR BUSINESS. The caption on this photograph proudly reads, "Our cook tent." The term *cook tent* is somewhat of a misnomer, since most of the cooking was actually done on a camp stove outside of the tent, for obvious reasons.

MAKING A HOME. This unusual photograph shows an unnamed soldier in the final stages of erecting his tent. Each of these pup tents housed two soldiers, and one wonders where his tent mate is when the heavy work needs to be done.

COLONEL HUME. The laconic caption for this photograph simply reads, "Col. Hume, 2nd Maine Inf." It would appear that he was one of the principal commanders of the red army. As such, he engineered this invasion of Newtown in his attempt to get across the county and into New York State.

THE COMPANY OFFICERS' TENT. The company officers included captains and first and second lieutenants. They commanded the small immediate group in which the photographer functioned and fought. This tent is substantially larger than the enlisted man's tent being pitched on the previous page—one of the many prerogatives of rank.

118

The Skirmish Line. This most extraordinary snapshot was taken while the photographer's company was charging across the field in formation. Action shots like this are extremely rare and only appear in army maneuvers when real ammunition is not being used. Getting this shot under actual battle conditions would have probably led to the photographer's death.

The Stretcher Bearers. Even in army maneuvers being conducted with blanks for ammunition, there are "casualties." It is uncertain exactly what the criteria were for becoming a casualty, but the whole operation was attended by a large number of umpires, and the job of determining the causalities undoubtedly fell to them.

THE AMBULANCE. The casualties were taken by the stretcher bearers to a dressing station and then evacuated in this ambulance. Many of the contemporary accounts of these week-long maneuvers tell that it was unbearably hot. It would have been a considerable relief for the wounded to lie for a while in the shade and then to be allowed to ride out of harm's way.

PATCHED UP. The dressing stations treated a large variety of fictitious wounds, as can be seen here. This part of the exercise was necessary to give medics, ambulance drivers, and other medical personnel experience under simulated battle conditions. The experience gained here was put to use five years later, when these men became part of a real army in the trenches of France.

BATTLE LINES FORMED. The first full-pitched battle occurred on Arcadia Farm on August 12 (see page 80). Caught in these Corbit postcards, the red army is drawn up in one of Homer Clark's cornfields ready to force back the blue army, which had arrived earlier that morning to contest any further progress toward the reservoirs.

HUNKERED DOWN. Photographer Lou Corbit caught this contingent of the blue army's 2nd Connecticut Infantry hunkered down behind a wall in Clark's barnyard. This was a defensive position that was soon overrun. Note the two boys standing on the wall in the upper right. Frequently, observers got in the way of the troop movement and even pitched battles. At the final skirmish, there were actually more observers than soldiers.

BLOODY LANE. This is either one of the casualties or, as is more likely, a soldier posed by Corbit for this scene, which is reminiscent of Matthew Brady's photographs taken at Gettysburg.

PRISONERS NEAR NEWTOWN. Just as in a real battle, prisoners were taken, except that here umpires determined when a position had been overrun and who the prisoners were. This photograph was taken on August 17, the last day of fighting. Since it was the military custom to move all prisoners to the rear, these troops may not even be in Newtown. The scenery does not appear to be local.

THE OBSERVERS. One of the objectives of these maneuvers, besides giving the U.S. Army's East Coast troops some fighting experience, was to show off the army and the latest developments in warfare, both in tactics and equipment. For this purpose, many dignitaries were invited to observe. Here, Massachusetts Governor Foss is standing in front of the Cole (later Gretsch) house on top of Castle Hill, overlooking the west side of the village.

THE OBSERVERS. These observers were actually in charge of the maneuvers. The commander of the U.S. Army in the Northeast was Brig. Gen. Trasker Bliss, seen here with his staff at Arcadia Farm. It was his job to set up the situation and arrange for the deployment of his troops. Once that was done, decisions on how the war would proceed were made by his subalterns, and he became an observer.

THE TROOPS IN REDDING. Initially, the blue army was spread all over Fairfield County, from Danbury to Bridgeport. As the maneuvers progressed, the troops became increasingly concentrated in the area around Newtown. This is the blue army artillery camp, located on the east bank of the Aspetuck River in Poverty Hollow (where Great Meadow Road is today).

THE TROOPS IN REDDING. The artillery park for the blue army was arranged just a short distance from the tents of the main Redding camp. This was one of the last stops before coming to Newtown for the final defense of the county.

THE TROOPS IN REDDING. These photographs were taken by some unrecorded member of the Hogeson family who lived on Poverty Hollow Road across form the entrance to Church Hill Road, and thus across the river from the camp. The photographer was fascinated by the personalities of the camp and its equipment. Here, Col. Dewitt Weld, commander of the blue army artillery, surveys the camp.

THE TROOPS IN REDDING. The presence of an army in Redding, something that had not happened since 1777 and the British raid on Danbury, created a great deal of interest among the people of Redding. The next day, as the troops marched out, many women, such as the one pictured to the left, came to the hollow to watch the parade.

THE TROOPS IN REDDING. As the supporting infantry marched up Poverty Hollow Road toward destiny, the artillery was being dragged up Church Hill Road. From there, it went on to Taunton Hill in Newtown and then to Coles Hill just west of the village. Later, on August 17, the blue army defended Coles Hill against the onslaught of the red army.

SPOTTING AIRCRAFT IN STRATFORD. This recently discovered photograph was taken at Camp Lee in Stratford by an unidentified photographer. The two spotting aircraft seen here were being used by the army for the first time. The spotter for the blue army flew over the red position, noting how the troops were deployed, and then returned to Paradise Green, where the information was sent by wireless to the blue army.

126

THE WIRELESS. The wireless was another piece of new technology that was being used for the first time by the army. This appears to be one of the mobile stations that would have followed the headquarters of either army. When the headquarters stopped, it would be set up to receive the latest aerial intelligence from Stratford.

WAITING FOR ORDERS. The red army troops are at ease in front of the Grand Central Hotel (later the Yankee Drover). When the order did arrive, these troops went up the hill against the blue army, which was defending the summit.

AFTER THE CLIMB AT HILL 698. This picture is a bit confusing, but it appears to have been taken after the battle of Coles Hill (Hill 698), with the troops of the red army at rest. This photograph was also part of the album that supplied the photographs at the beginning of this chapter. The battle here was declared a victory for the red army by the umpires, so these troops rest here, exultant in victory.

CONFUSION AFTER THE BATTLE. While the victorious red army rested to the south, the right flank, on Mount Pleasant, was running into much heavier resistance that it had anticipated and the umpires declared a blue army victory. In the end, the battle was called a draw and the troops emerged from the confusion seen here to head to all of the towns' railroad depots, where they embarked for home.

.

www.ingramcontent.com/pod-product-compliance
Lightning Source LLC
Chambersburg PA
CBHW050707110426
42813CB00007B/2108